ALONG THE HEAVENLY HIGHWAY

BY

LESLIE JORDAN

ISBN: 1-4107-9241-2 (e-book)
ISBN: 1-4107-9240-4 (Paperback)

This book is printed on acid free paper.

1stBooks - rev. 10/28/03

TABLE OF CONTENTS

INTRODUCTION

Welcome to the Heavenly Highway

Everyone it seems is looking for one magic answer to transform life and make their world a better place. Life abundant with great peace is the goal. People are willing, even anxious, to try just about anything to experience improvement in their lives. The goal is for something to make them into all they wish they were. Romans 8:4-6 speaks to this impulse; "That the righteousness of the law might be fulfilled in us, who walk not after the flesh, but after the Spirit. For they that are after the flesh do mind the things of the flesh; but they that are after the Spirit the things of the Spirit. For to be carnally minded is death; but to be spiritually minded is life and peace." In these inspired words from a loving Father to confused children is the answer; the life and peace men seek. By being spiritually minded, minding the things of the spirit, the physical life can become rich and full. In the majestic book of Isaiah 32:17,18 are these comforting and assuring words from our Father, "And the work of righteousness shall be peace; and the effect of righteousness quietness and assurance for ever. And my people shall dwell in a peaceable habitation, and in sure dwellings, and in quiet resting places."

From the moment we give our hearts to the Lord, when Christ takes up dwelling in our souls, we begin a journey along the heavenly highway. The Bible, God's Word, is the guide giving direction, help, instruction, encouragement, and hope for the new walk with Christ. Through the pages of God's Word is found victory to overcome Satan's assaults. By fulfilling the righteousness of the law in walking after the Spirit, the Father will grant joy for the journey walked hand in hand with His Son. Since the beginning of time God has remained the same while mankind has struggled to find the will of God for his life. Why is it we always must complicate matters? On the pages following we will look at and consider the day by day walk with Christ. By allowing the Lord within you to speak to you and give direction, you will keep close by the side of the Savior, you can make a lasting difference in the world around you. Go ahead and exercise the faith God has given. As you listen to the guide inside your heart, and reach out more to others, you may find it becomes more comfortable to reach upward toward God. Hopefully the pages here will prove to be an encouragement and a help to those traveling this wonderful path along the heavenly highway.

There is nothing startling or new to be found here, nothing magic, no secret newly found. A pot of gold with a little green leprechaun to grant wishes is fantasy and unreal. The yellow brick road leading to the enchanted city is fantasy. The path with God however, is very real. The path of the heavenly highway promises companionship, and a secure assurance of fulfillment that can be found on no other path. For no one walks alone here; the Savior always is near, the sweet Holy Spirit remains in our heart and in our life. You will be encouraged to act and live according to God's will. There are many Christians walking along this heavenly highway. You will meet people of every age and color and level of society and every level of education. The way appears very difficult and filled with struggle for some travelers who have not realized the peace they could have, for some life is lonely, enough to cause them to consider dropping from the path. These people need a helping hand to remind them we are never alone. Testimony is seen and heard whereby we are encouraged by great overcoming grace; testimony of endurance with joy unspeakable in time of trial. Such testimony will strengthen others to go on, try again. Then also are times walking a lonely valley in a darkened hour where we see no one, hear nothing. Satan might whisper to you no one is near, no one cares; but he can only tell untruths. Remember the Word.

Do not despair, you are not alone. (Hebrews 13:5, "for he hath said, I will never leave thee, nor forsake thee."), no trial is so great God will not be able to meet the need. No, He is ever able and always willing to be your sufficiency. There is power to be found in a fully dedicated child of God who has been filled with and is now led by the Holy Spirit. To each of His children God offers power and grace. Thankful indeed are those children who accept this good offer. Peace that passes understanding is exactly as stated; one could never understand where peace comes from in the midst of a raging storm. One of the wonderful things about this heavenly highway journey is realizing there are so many great truths to learn, precious times with the Lord to enjoy, you will marvel that you are able to contain all the wonders and goodness and love our Lord will bestow upon you.

So take in hand your Bible, God's Word, as your help and guide and book of life's instruction. Accept the offer of God your Father, and walk in new light each day. Set out today in great anticipation and excitement for the journey God has planned. Remember with each new day, whatever that day may bring, it takes you one step closer to that final destination to stand in the presence of the King of all Kings. In fact the journey takes you along the highway with the King now that He has dwelt within your heart. You can know great joy along the way because you are new, born into a new creature. Paul assured us in Romans 8:35-39 we will not be separated from the love of God and we are conquerors through him Who loved us. You will find your way in the pages of God's Word. Each day expect to know the hand of God is leading, keeping and guiding you.

May your heavenly journey be one of inspiration calling others to the way of truth and light. May you know great blessing as you travel your own journey along the Heavenly Highway.

WONDERFUL, MARVELOUS, AMAZING GRACE

Wonderful, Marvelous, Amazing Grace!
Twas amazing grace that cleansed my soul,
Amazing grace that made me whole.
Amazing that His grace set free,
Once sin blind eyes now glory see.
Lame, undone, poor and alone;
That blood for sinners did atone.
Amazing grace that Christ our King,
Would cause our broken hearts to sing.
It shall forever be my song,
Till one day midst that heavenly throng,
I cast myself before His feet,
To thank Him for that grace so sweet.

Wonderful, Marvelous, Amazing Grace!

(LMJ)

1

KNOW CHRIST ON THE HEAVENLY HIGHWAY

"These things have I written unto you that believe on the name of the Son of God; that ye may know that ye have eternal life, and that ye may believe on the name of the Son of God." I John 5:13

"And we know that the Son of God is come, and hath given us an understanding, that we may know him that is true, and we are in him that is true, even in his son, Jesus Christ, this is the true God, and eternal life." I John 5:20

Knowing Jesus Christ is the very foundation of your life, and of your being. Upon this foundation is built the hope of help both here and for all eternity. Proverbs 1:7a, "The fear of the Lord is the beginning of knowledge..." It is the firm foundation of knowing and believing His Word from which we may gain wisdom.

All wisdom is from God. Since this is a basic fact, here would be a good place to begin. In constructing a building the foundation must be engineered and set in place before any other work on the structure

3

may begin. Careful detail is made to ensure the foundation will safely hold the planned building. Wisdom from God is your foundation on which to build. Be very sure of your place in Christ, know your heart has been cleansed by the blood of Christ; know your sins have been forgiven. There will be many things you will want to know, but above all, know you are a child of God. From this basis and from this knowledge will come your hope, and joy and peace, power, victory, and help for living.

In the book of John are golden words guiding us to knowledge. John 3:7, "Marvel not that I said unto thee, ye must be born again." Do not be fooled by morality, or what seems to be a good appearance. People are gullible, it is easy to fool others into believing something quite untrue; at least for awhile. Being moral, hardworking, or looking good does not save you. Salvation is only accomplished through faith by the blood of Christ and the full acceptance of His Word. We must open the door of our heart and allow the Holy Spirit entrance. God will make of us a new creation, the old will pass, and the new is born. Hence the term, "born again".

"That whosoever believeth in him should not perish, but have eternal life." John 3:15 The promise is one in which we may rest assured for all of our life. Watching some Christians it appears they believe they must wait until after death to be with Christ. But if Christ be in us, we live with Him now; He lives with and in us. Eternal life has already begun. Upon realizing the truth of His indwelling Holy Spirit our daily life will show God's love and power.

There is a place of sweet fellowship, great peace and deep abiding faith. Not in some far off time or some far away location; but within the heart and mind of the believer. These are the things giving God's children strength and power. These are the weapons of warfare to battle the enemy. Be warned however, should sin have crept into the life and heart of a believer, the place of fellowship, and peace and faith moves farther and farther away. Consider this, that sin is the great divider. Satan is the great deceiver. Never forget that, or that he is powerful and subtle. Satan wants you to lose the victory and joy and peace God has given you. He will continually try to battle you and harass you and weary you.

However, he is not all powerful. Though his power is great, Satan knows he is already a defeated foe. You have to remember he is already defeated. God alone has all power. We do indeed have a formidable foe. But there is also a mighty conqueror at our side! The foe would have you believe there is no chance for victory in life. Yet the more you know Christ and know of Him, the more you will clearly see Satan as the wicked defeated foe. Defeated is the key word here, it is a cause for continual praise. An underlying truth lies here affecting all of the problems of life. Sin against God and His Word is the real core problem with every troubled heart; every confused mind, every broken life, every broken home. Sin will manifest itself as murder, and rape, robbery, violence, adultery, gossip, backbiting, hatred. Do you notice even the word "sin" is distasteful to speak? The blood of Christ is the only thing able to cleanse sin bringing the troubled sinner to the place of peace and hope of God. As God's

5

child you have a shield against Satan. Without Christ and His cleansing blood the battle would be constant. Satan stirs up the flesh of the world and creates havoc any way he can.

Satan may send trouble your way but you have an adversary and you have holy armor. Victory and joy is exactly what our Father wants for our life. Once the decision is made to accept God and His Word, it will encourage the child of God to stand on the faith now living in him. In standing there is faith for walking, walking a daily life for and with Jesus Christ. Reading God's Word daily will reassure the child of God of grace and strength for every trial. We know, because God told us, we will not ever be alone. Are these not great truths to know?

Once you know without doubt that you are in Christ; you embark on a wonderful and joyful journey of power and victory and deep assurance through life right into eternity with our lovely Lord. Keep yourself close by Him, you will rest in heavenly places. Expect to have joy now, in this life, today, it is eternal; expect the joy to have begun. Eternal you know indicates neither beginning nor end. It is possible to walk along the road of life at a level unknown to anyone outside of Christ and His promises. You are founded on a sure foundation, and nothing can shake you from your faith. Such is the strength God gives to His child. Christianity is not a contrived faith leading followers off into a mist to find seclusion or mystic isolation. This is a faith that lives and works.

Having found so practical a faith you will affect the community around you. The knowledge of God in your life will give you the kind of changed life that has to be seen. It is a faith that reaches the lost, the needy, and the poor in spirit. You can be a vital part of the world around you. God gives a faith that draws people, a faith that makes people feel secure around you. Most definitely you can know you are in Christ and you can know Who Christ is.

Some things that reveal I know Christ:

Perhaps you would like to take some time on this page and jot down notes as to what your life and heart indicate about your working knowledge of Christ.

Christ's place in my heart_____

Christ's place in my home_____

Christ' place in my church life _____

Christ's place in my work or job_____

Christ's place in my social life _____

Areas to pray for God's help _____

ENCOURAGING ALONG THE HEAVENLY HIGHWAY

The team is on the field, rain falls, deepening the chill of the night. Weary players view the scoreboard to verify they still lag behind the visiting team. What a long game! About then cheers begin coming out of the stands, the exuberant cheerleaders leap and wave their pom poms and vault through the air in excitement for the team. One by one the players catch the energy of the cheers as they resound from the stands; hey, we can do this, we can score, we can win! Encouragement spurs them on with new energy.

Everyone needs encouraging at times. Man was made to interact, to be part of one another's lives. No one is intended to walk alone on the journey of life. "No man is an island entire in himself; every man is a part of the whole, a piece of the main". The journey through life, when it involves guidance and fellowship with Christ the Savior, is more precious than gold. Yet, sometimes even in such a blessed state,

9

a feeling of discouragement may creep in. Discouragement creeps in on pastors, on teachers, on joyful singers, on the young people, on the children, the fathers, mothers, working women, toiling men, on everyone at one time or another. There is great blessing and sweet fellowship along the heavenly way; there will also be labor which may wear out the soul and body. At times there may be discouragement when we have been misunderstood or physical weakness when we are taken ill. These things can cause a depressing attitude. In the midst of such a time encouragement from a brother or sister in Christ makes a difference to help endure. Just like the cheers at a game. Everybody needs encouragement, when you do not need the help yourself; look around you for someone who needs you to encourage them. If you are a child of God, you know He is ever living within your heart; a little touch in a tough time will remind you to allow Him to be your strength.

In Deuteronomy 1:38 and in 3:28 the Israelites were told to encourage Joshua as their leader in order that he might lead them. Time has yet to change the fact; leaders still need help and encouragement. Leadership carries with it great responsibility. Those who follow have the responsibility to pray for and encourage and obey the command of their leaders. Those who follow such a teaching make the whole body of Christ move forward with a more sure purpose as the people pray for one another. How often do we remember to encourage our pastor, or our state or our national leaders? They seem so large and important to us we find them remote and even unreal to our life. But they are just men and women and they feel the same as we do. One Sunday our pastor brought a message that was full of patriotism for our great country and admiration for the office of President and for our then current President, Ronald Reagan. As I listened I thought people do not hesitate to send angry or complaining messages to our leaders, why not send a positive message? The tape of that message was sent with a note to the White House with an encouraging note for the President. That was the last I expected to hear of it or think of the action. Later a reply came thanking me for the inspirational message. "The President appreciates the spiritual sentiments which prompted you to take the time to remember him in such a special way. Messages such as yours help make his task easier. With the President's best wishes, Anne Higgins, Special Assistant to the President and Director of Correspondence." What a nice feeling to know it did matter to make a kind gesture.

Everyone needs to feel encouraged. As a Christian the love of God is in our heart, as is His strength, His peace, His joy; we are to be a fountain not a cistern. The water of life must flow freely through the Christian. It only takes a moment, a very small thing, a hug and a smile to make the difference in a tough day for someone. A great thing about being an encourager of others is that every time you reach out to encourage someone you are reaching yourself too. Everyone benefits so it is a wonderful plan. The more often you are encouraging the more you will know how to take care of yourself through Christ. Perhaps the Holy Spirit within our heart feels He has more freedom to move and work through us as we reach out!

11

David, in I Samuel 30:6 found himself in a terrible situation. His wives had been taken captive, people wanted to stone him, he was greatly distressed. Now notice this, "...but David encouraged himself in the Lord". There was no one else at that time to lift him up, but David knew God was able and he knew how to get to God for help. Knowledge of where to find help and encouragement is essential as the journey continues, for distress will sometimes come. You may have someone who will reach out to you, or there may not be anyone to help. At such a time you need to get to God by yourself. In Christ there is hope and there is help.

It may be that you will be walking along on your journey through life weary from toil, moving slowly now. There is no energy that could be put into the current problem. All of a sudden you realize some other person is struggling and it seems they may not be able to continue, they may fall away. At this time, even though you are so weary, you feel their need. God guides you go to them and take their hand, to strengthen their feeble knees. A surge of energy goes through you as God the Father smiles at the sight and sound of His child living in obedience. With this new burst of energy, you are not feeling weary now; you have strength to spare for this weak brother or sister. Hebrews 12:12 "Wherefore lift up the hands which hang down, and the feeble knees." What mighty power is available in His name!

Nothing can compare to the blessing of being a blessing to others. It is in such times we are most like Jesus. He gave all for us, could we not give a little? In the times of helping and serving and giving of ourselves we experience a little bit of what it is to be Christ like. When The Holy Spirit moved into our heart we became a new creature, with His way within our heart it will be natural to do His will. Being a blessing, being an encourager is a very precious thing. Encouraging one who does not know Christ may help them know their need of the Savior. Why don't you ask God to help you see the need in those around you; try asking Him to show you how you can help them; and in doing so He will show you how to be more like Jesus. Your walk will be brighter and more full than you can ever imagine. Like the cheerleaders pulling their team back to the work at hand, reach out and cheer someone on the way. Be an encourager to others to live like Jesus, help others to allow the Lord to free them to have victory.

WHY DID GOD ALLOW HARD THINGS ALONG THE HEAVENLY HIGHWAY?

Far too early in the morning the alarm rings, turn it off, roll out of bed. Ouch! Step on the hot wheels car you could not find after your child went to bed. Stagger into the bathroom, accidentally bump into the door jamb, miss the light switch the first couple of tries, splash water on your face and knock three items onto the floor reaching for the towel. A new day has begun! Looks like it may take some time to get to "This is the day that the Lord hath made". What is wrong with you? Probably nothing, life is just not always as we want it to be. Little things create interference in every life. Grace takes over and helps us to deal with them when we know the Savior. Sometimes it becomes almost comical trying to make life run smoothly. How do all these inanimate objects have a vengeance against us? Of course they do not and we learn to deal with daily life and the usual stress. However, all around us are instances of much more serious situations.

Every day there are reports of terrible and frightening circumstances in the lives of good people. Dreadful disease spreads, people lose their control, violence erupts, injuries occur; auto accidents occur every minute, every second. In the news we hear and read of wars all over the globe and terrorism is going on and on. Babies are born pre-mature, sick and weak, good Christian people have nervous breakdowns, marriages fall apart, children choose a life of sin rather than live for God. There is an overwhelming mountain of despair in the news. Our world appears to be run by a whirling dervish. Why did God allow all of these hard things? How could all of this be happening?

The person in a crisis is surrounded by "friends" with advice: "God will use the hard things in your life to strengthen you, you will grow by this." "God gives troubles to those He knows can handle it." "The closer we get to His coming, the worse the world will be." "Everybody has troubles of some kind, you have to be strong and trust Him." These are some of the usual comments of counsel offered in troubling times. "God had a reason for this trouble." Well, did He? Or perhaps could God, our Father, have preferred there be no trouble? Our Father always wants what is good for His children.

In Deuteronomy 28:58 & 60, Moses wrote, "If thou wilt not observe to do all the words of this law that are written in this book, that thou mayest fear this glorious and fearful name, THE LORD THY GOD; Moreover he will bring upon thee all the diseases of Egypt, which thou was afraid of; and they shall cleave unto thee." The children of Israel refused to continue following their God.

16

Finally they were scattered and are still today found among every nation. Everywhere they have been persecuted. Christians are the children of Abraham, the children of that same God. Could they expect His best blessings if His Word is not obeyed? Is God different today? He is not.

For an example of the foolishness of people consider this. New strains of flu and viral infections spread like wildfire. We may be making our own troubles, not having them "given" to us. All the way back to the time of the Old Testament Leviticus instructs the people of God to separate those that are sick, those with wounds that run, those with contagious disease. Anyone touching any of their clothing, or person, or bedding, or chair on which they sat, was to wash himself well. The sick person was to continually wash themselves. Lev.15:9 goes so far as to insist to clean even the saddle, to consider it unclean. The Bible instructed to use running water, as it would be more pure, to do so for seven days. Read Lev. chapters 15 and 22, very interesting. What kind of a difference could be seen during "flu season" if each parent just kept their child isolated and clean, with clean bedding every day - remember all those germs they emit are on the pillow and bed and on their night clothes. Even the simple act of washing hands which should be habit to wash with great frequency is often neglected. If you know that you have a viral disease, whatever it is, you do not have to spread it. If your child has something contagious, don't spread it. Have a fever? Stay away from others. The Word of God is ever practical and applicable to all areas of life.

God's law had to be broken several times for such a thing as HIV to get started and to continue to spread. Though research is needed now, a better answer to the problem would be the practice of holy living by God's children. Should we decide to ignore the Word of God and His way then we will reap the rewards of sin. Ignoring or disagreeing does not change what God said. Man may choose to ignore all he wants to; God changes not.

Ignorance of God's Word or disregard of that Word is at the root of most, if not all the dire straits into which people fall. Unfortunately these situations are common. People claiming to know Christ watch television talk shows and panel shows of people with colorful and dramatic troubles, then take the suggestions of the world for their life. When is the time they read the Word of God, and think about, Philippians 4:8 & 9? "...whatsoever things are lovely...think on these things..." Such reminder and hope from the Scripture could make a difference. A difference in daily decisions.

A real difference could be made in your home, social circle, job, town, even state and nation. Why do God's people even listen to what the media feeds us? Paul said in Ephesians 5:12, "For it is a shame even to speak of those things which are done of them in secret." Today people take "those things" and amplify them for entertainment. Then as we go to sleep we ask our heavenly Father to bless our lives! Do you wonder if He groans sometimes? It could be a great blessing to the community if God's children made a commitment to live according to the Word He gave.

In order to live in victory and strength of course it will take a Christian stronger than one who merely talks about Christianity. Perhaps a person listens to a Christian radio station, maybe reads their Bible a little each day, and attends church in a more or less regular pattern. More is required for life changing. For real change there must be involved that so difficult word - discipline. Discipline in all areas of our lives. It is so hard on the flesh, but what rewards could be seen. Often it is difficult even to keep a child with a fever home and cared for; we have to shop, or take them to church and give it to the other children. Not much of a blessing there. Possibly while the child has a lower immunity from the illness they may catch something even more serious. Next we wonder why God allowed such a thing as this illness in our child. He didn't. For another example; we speed in our car, cut a corner, wander into the other lane, or commit some other driving error; then - a wreck. Someone is badly hurt. Why did God allow this? He didn't; God would like you to obey the law, drive carefully, and pay attention. You see, every area of life is affected by our obedience to God's Word. It is your choice to love God and walk with Him, or not walk with Him. Is the Holy Spirit in your heart trying to tell you the right way for your life? Will you listen to Him? There will be plenty of Satan's children to create problems and illness and challenges without God's children getting in on the action. True, you can't stop everything, everyone does not love God, and not everyone will hear you. But you can be different. Remember that when you were born again, you became a new creature. The old has been taken away and replaced with the new. Give this new Spirit room and freedom to grow and live. You never know who may be influenced by your testimony or whose life may be touched. You can, however, be certain some life will be affected by the way you lead your life. All you are will guide you in all you do. Ultimately, what is said is overshadowed by what is done; the walk will speak more loudly than the talk. Any area of life will prove this fact. Certainly the Bible promises we can make the difference for our own life and our family. Deuteronomy 6:5, 6.

"And thou shalt love the Lord thy God with all thine heart, and with all thy soul, and with all thy might. And these words, which I command thee this day, shall be in thine heart."

The more God and the Word of God is found in the life and heart of His children, the more consolation people will find during the hard things of their life.

GRACE'LL MAKE YOU TOUGH

When Satan's loathsome fiery dart,
Pierces deep within our heart.
You wince and cry aloud in pain
And wonder if your life's in vain.
You call out, "Father, it is enough!"
He says, "Hang on, grace'll make you tough."

This isn't how I hoped 'twould be,
When asking Him to strengthen me.
Where is the rainbow in the sky?
Where are the dreams for which I sigh?
I didn't know life was so gruff.
And yet he says, "Grace'll make you tough."

Yes, grace that soothes our fears and tears.
That keeps us true for all our years.
It is sufficient for your need.
If God's own word you will just heed.
So hang on Honey, it could get rough.
But its so true - Grace'll make you tough!

(LMJ)

21

THE SONGS IN YOUR HEART ALONG THE HEAVENLY HIGHWAY

Hearts are touched by music; let yours be touched and moved by the songs we love. Music can fill empty waiting minutes and keep nerves steady. It is not so long to wait for a medical test, for instance, if you are humming something like "Surely goodness and Mercy", or "Amazing Grace". A crashing thunderstorm will not seem so frightening to the children if they hear you singing, "My Anchor Holds", or "Living by Faith", as thunder crashes and winds blow. The story is told that on the ship sailing to America the songs of the Moravians on the turbulent seas touched the questioning heart of John Wesley. When your little one seems high-strung, or loud, and agitated, try putting on a tape of children's hymns, or even a quiet instrumental tape of sacred concert to help calm them. Notice what a calming effect it can have. Do you recall how David used his music to soothe King Saul? Music will help you and it will impact the children. We are told, "Let this mind be in you, as was also in Christ Jesus." (Phil.2:5) Probably you have noticed it is often difficult to have our mind in Christ Jesus. So much presses us, crowds our thoughts; we need help. Christ is our help; we know He is we just have trouble getting to Him. Some days too much of life is in the way to even be able to pray effectively. Music is a wonderful tool to use to move some heavy "stuff" out of the way, so that we can once again see Jesus.

When Jesus Christ is the song you sing, then in your heart rings music of victory and joy. The song will radiate from you as a warm glow. No one sings like the child of God. Throughout history God's people have been known for their song. Hearts full of God's Word and His love are happy, peaceful, singing hearts. The world knows many kinds of music, great talent, great voices; but none are able to touch a heart in the way of the songs of faith. Did you ever hear Mahaliah Jackson sing of her Savior in that rich full voice? Or have you listened to George Beverly Shea sing "How Great thou Art"? Such music has a depth matched by no other. The child of God sings of eternal foundational truths. The only music that can begin to compare at all are songs of battle as hearts on fire for victory go into war. Theirs is a cause that unifies the people, the songs and the passion promise victory and strength. Christians also go forth to battle; unified, encouraged, and strengthened by great old songs of the faith. The outcome of battle is sure, our victory has already been won, we sing in strength and joy and thankfulness.

Music plays a significant role in life. The various types of music heard throughout the day will influence thoughts and actions and attitudes even though it may go unnoticed in the background. Magazine articles have noted that some dining establishments will play peppy, move along music during the busy lunch hour to get people up and out. Some music excites and promotes activity or excitement; some is quieting, soothing and restful. Sometimes music is irritating or intrusive. Loud, driving, music with mournful lyrics can make it difficult to go about business. It is more difficult to keep your mind on everything you need to remember. I often feel it would be better for stores to play some sort of instrumental music, rather than what we usually hear. Sometimes you just want to get out of the place and get a break from the racket. Stores, offices, restaurants, even hold time on the telephone; all use music to fill a gap. I feel sometimes my mind needs to be brushed out after I've heard some part of a silly, empty song in a store and can not get it out of my mind.

Hearing a song sometimes brings back memories of a special time. Songs from childhood may bring back memories of being cared for and taught and loved, memories of celebrations with the family. Perhaps your Mother or Grandmother rocked you as a little one and sang Rock of Ages, or Sweet Hour of Prayer, or Jesus Loves Me. Singing these over as you are an adult will bring a bit of sweet memory to mind. An old hymn not heard for a long time may remind of earlier commitments and times of blessing with God. Every time the congregation sings "I Stand Amazed in the Presence", I remember Ashton Welch, a friend and the father of a dear friend from years back. We stood in some of the first services attended in our marriage with Ashton and his wife and often sang this song. It reminds me of the fresh new feeling of being in God's house and seeing people that served God faithfully many years. Their influence still remains. Music may be a reminder of the teaching of a pastor who taught of the Good Shepherd leading the way to righteousness. Somewhere in the mind and the heart the blessed old songs learned years ago remain, to be pulled back out now and then for their sweet savor.

There may come a time when sin has crept into life; how comforting then, after asking God's forgiveness, to be able to sing a song like, "Grace Greater Than Our Sin". "Marvelous grace of our loving Lord, Grace that exceeds our sin and our guilt, Yonder on Calvary's mount out-poured, there where the blood of the Lamb was spilt." The singing of such a powerful message is bound to make a heart feel stronger. No one else has the peace and joy experienced by God's child. Singing the songs of faith will insure more stability and help; such a practice will mean much less opportunity for depression. I am not a scientist, nor a medical expert; but I have found it to be true that it is impossible to murmur, complain, or grouch at the same time you are singing a song of praise! Satan does not like to be around joyful music, he will leave if you continue to sing of the blood of Christ. Once he has left, you are bound to feel better!

God has given a full arsenal with which to battle Satan. Look in the book of Ephesians at the wonderful amour provided. Satan and his imps seem strong, which they are; but never so strong as is the great God Jehovah! The child of God has full armor, effective weapons, a sure battle plan, a great hope, an established end; and best of all, the Captain of the Lord of Hosts to fight for us. Unfortunately the soldiers in God's army seem to occasionally forget about one or another piece of the amour. How can such a thing happen? Could you imagine a Marine forgetting some vital part of his combat pack as he rushes into battle? A very unlikely thought. Perhaps the Christian is not so serious about the battle as is the Marine?

For the battles of life there are weapons and material given to help. Of those things given for our help music is an important part. Godly music is a powerful tool. For myself, on a day when I am feeling bad or things have been more stressful than usual I have a few favorite songs I sing all by myself alone as I drive in my truck. Songs like "Satisfied", and "Feeling Mighty Fine" and "Oh The Glory did Roll", songs that give me strength and renewal. They are songs that are fun to sing and I like to sing them louder than the devil can talk to me! The music of God's children has been greatly used through all time. Remember reading of the late night singing in the jail when Paul and Silas had been arrested? And at another time when the capturing army asked the Israelites to sing their songs? Remember even in our country's history how the soldiers on both sides of the Civil War sang? There have been numerous war stories told of the singing of the soldiers overseas in World War I and II. God knows we need a song in our heart. He has given many wonderful songs over the years to people to pass along as a help. These precious melodies draw Christians together, they help to give us expression of our worship and prepare hearts for the Word that will be preached, and they encourage the weary hearts.

Customarily a service will begin with music. There may be a variety of old hymns, a chorus or two, joyful songs of testimony, songs of praise and worship. Minds are helped by the songs to become quiet and steady, open to hear the Word of God. Hearts become touched and softened, and moved toward God and His Word. Some of the music thrills us as we remember how we were saved and changed by grace. Sometimes the music causes a deep seriousness at the realization of what is required of the child of God. Always the music has a definite impact on the service, on the hearts of the people. Enjoy the music, worship God and his love as you sing, put your heart into it and the song will touch others. Even for the very young or for the visitor unfamiliar with the teachings of the Bible, the songs of faith touch someplace deep in hearts as nothing else could do. One time I took with me to an evening service a young woman who was not accustomed to church services. She had been my physical therapist at the hospital where I was being treated and God had given opportunity to talk with her. As Marylou sat watching the congregation and listening to everything, her curiosity about everything was obvious. A trio of ladies began to sing "Precious Jesus, sweet rose of Sharon". Their voices blended beautifully, and they conveyed well the message of the song. Marylou's eyes filled with tears as she listened. Leaning toward me she said, "What is it about that song? I am so moved by it?" With her heart softened, God's Word found an easier ground in which to plant truth.

Now it goes without saying that these women had great sincerity, and put a lot into their song. The congregation as well that night seemed to sing with real feeling. Think for a moment; how often during the singing in a service do you think about the message of a song? How many of the songs do you know without the book? Perhaps you already know that singing the songs of our faith in your home, as you go about your daily business, deepens your faith. To burst into even a short segment of a song of praise during the day will brighten the day and bring refreshment. It is a little bit like holding on to the rail as you climb steep stairs. By your practice in front of them do your children know the songs of their faith? For instance, do you and your children know all the words to "When I See The Blood"? Do you sing it as you work, or garden, or drive, or cook? What about "My Jesus I Love Thee"? This is a beautiful hymn, one that helps the child of God worship. Many songs could be listed here; these are only a tiny example. Hiding the Word of God in our heart is our foundation; keeping the songs of faith and praise in our heart is like the open windows letting in fresh breezes to refresh.

Perhaps you are a new Christian, or perhaps you never thought much about any need to sing or use these songs away from church. Whether you feel you sing well is of no matter. A lot of people seem to think most of what is done in church, the Bible reading, singing, praying, fellowshipping; is to be done only on Sunday and only at the church. Nothing could be further from the truth. May I recommend to you that you need the music of your faith in all areas of your life. Get some tapes and compact disks to listen to with good music of the faith, learn the words, get out a song book and sing a couple of songs. Teach them to your children. They probably would like to hear you sing. Especially if your children have heard you are a griper or sharp tongued more than a singer of happy songs! The songs your children learn will stay with them all their lives, and will help them. Some time ago I was waiting to have our car inspected; two more people were before me. It was hot so all of us waiting had gotten out of our vehicle and stood beside them. Nearby a man probably in his late fifties leaned against his pickup. He was unshaven, face deeply lined, coarse and weary looking. As I stood by the car I whistled, absent mindedly, an old gospel tune called "The Glory Did Roll". The man walked over to me, "Hey, I know that song!" he said, "I used to hear that at some meetings my grandmother took me to when I was a kid." For a few minutes we visited about the old meetings, the songs, the preachers. You see, just the sound of a song the man had not heard in years opened a door of remembrance in his heart. Perhaps God was able to touch the man and remind him of some of the other things he heard at those old meetings.

Music of the faith can act as a filter of sorts. Try it in your home and life. If you have no song book, get one. There may be an old one around your church - if you ask. Let's not just take home a book without asking. Bookstores carry songbooks and hymnbooks, Salvation Army and Goodwill stores have a book section and frequently have some music books. Every home should have a couple of hymn books. At least read the words aloud even if you don't sing them. Encourage the children to read the beautiful verses aloud; it is a great training tool. For our son Todd's thirty second birthday he said what he wanted was to have all of his favorite people come over to get around the old piano and sing all evening. They did, and everyone ate, and visited and sang, the kids played and were in and out; all in all it was a great time. Everyone went home happy and ready to rest and meet another day.

In order to grow in grace and learn more of Christ it will take all of the tools and all of the directions God has given. Be careful not to neglect this one very important tool. More than just a tool, the music of our great faith is a true joy and benefit, a wonderful gift. God has given us so very much, always meeting our needs. No wonder His child will want to sing, "I Love To Tell The Story". Remember, it is nearly impossible to complain or gripe, and sing at the same time? When you feel alone and fearful sing or hum the song, "Never Alone". Or at a time when things are not going as you would like them to and you may be concerned about what will happen tomorrow, try "I Don't Know About Tomorrow". So perhaps next time there is a temptation to be grouching, a song of joy would change the air. Play recordings of worshipful music as you work and perform your daily tasks; it will enrich your life and help keep your mind tuned to the Lord when He speaks to you. Learn to love the songs of your faith; make them a part of your life. You will be enriched by the beauty and hope and love good music will bring to your life. "The joy of the Lord is my strength", wrote Nehemiah, we sing this as a chorus and it will indeed give strength. Let us express that joy and increase our strength.

31

WITH OUR CHILDREN ON THE HEAVENLY HIGHWAY

"Thus saith the Lord; Refrain thy voice from weeping, and thine eyes from tears; for thy work shall be rewarded, saith the Lord; and they shall come again from the land of the enemy. And there is hope in thine end, saith the Lord that thy children shall come again to their own border." Jeremiah 31:16, 17

What a tremendous promise of hope! Traveling along this Heavenly Highway we know to keep our children held up in prayer. Children are a source of great joy; they complete a couple, a home and family. Children can also be a source of great frustration, perhaps tears shed; a reason for much labor and toil. After all they represent a fulfillment of much that is good and also perhaps what is not so good in us. There are so many details to worry about, to teach, be an example, etc. one may neglect to take the time needed to just enjoy the kids. Our children are first a gift from God, they also are a

33

continuation of us and our family, they are a source of abiding hope. Each child is a little like a tapestry with silken threads from many sources making up their personality. A little of Dad, of Mom, and grandparents on both sides, a little of an aunt or an uncle, traits and talents pop up from who knows how far back in the line. Such dreams and hope we have for the tiny new bundle of life when the baby arrives in our home!

Over forty years ago now our first child came into our lives. I was not far from a child myself, getting married at just seventeen then in eleven months this beautiful little baby girl is a part of my life. First babies born to very young mothers have to have a special toughness I think. It is amazing how little I knew, and my mother had already gone to be with the Lord. But Janet was healthy and bright and together we grew. Along the way three little boys arrived and finally one more little girl. With sixteen years between the girls they in a way had different mothers. Jim and I did not try to follow God's Word early on in our home, we loved the children and cared for them, but God had no prominent place as yet. That came after several years. Their father worked hard and was steady and I was able to be home with them, so we had a lot of time together. Our home was in a quiet little New Hampshire town set on a country road. It was a nice place for children to live and play; they did not have too many conflicting influences to confuse them. Living in a large urban area like Houston where the younger ones finished growing up creates perhaps greater challenges. Location however is probably not as critical to the children as the state of the parent's heart and mind. You never know what changes life will bring about. Looking back remembering it seems those earlier times were simpler times. Today life seems more complicated.

Parents naturally worry about children as they try to raise them, especially when the teen years arrive with those special challenges and all of the questions about life that come up. Before you realize time has gone so quickly, it is on to college and career. God tells us in his Word, "fear not", "weep not", "take no thought", "have no care". God tries through His Word to show His children a clear safe path for parenting and lead them away from painful stress and worry. Do His children take heed? No, not very often it seems. Of course if the parents have made their mind up to listen to the Spirit of Christ in their heart they are way ahead of many others who like aimless sheep wander into danger. The concerned parent does not want their child to be victim to unwise decisions and choices. It would be nice to keep our children from having to pay the cost of unwise decisions. But our beloved offspring may not listen, as the parent did not listen to the grandparent. Puzzled and perplexed the parent seeks an answer, of some sort to explain what appears to be a display of ignorance. This helpless babe you carried and trained and held by the hand through early learning years now seeks a full independence. It was a hard thing to let go of the babe for those first early steps. It never gets easier to let go. But letting go is how they learned to walk. And letting go is a part of maturity and growth as well.

A good parent needs to maintain a prayerful watchfulness throughout the child's life. In that the parent is responsible for the training and safety of the child, it behooves Mom and Dad to pay attention to their child. Have you ever thought about just who is this child of yours? How well do you know the child and their interests? What kind of person is your child? Who are his friends? What are the areas of his interests? How would you as a parent know if your child did have a problem, would you see the difference in his, or her, actions and disposition? Can you tell if your child is hurt, or troubled, or excited? You may have a great young person living in your house that you do not even know very well.

What a shame to miss out on the blessing of a real relationship together while the child is young. We spent some time working with girls that needed some special help, and had to be away from their homes for awhile. So many of these girls would say there was seldom anyone to talk to them, their parents were too busy, or gone. Children need you far more than they need what you work to buy. New carpet won't help a lonely child. Take the time to get to know each child, talk to them, and listen to them. Be interested in what your children have to say, what do they think about? Let your child know that in your home is someone that cares about them and their thoughts. The rewards of caring for the child stay with you both forever.

In our family after we had all five of our children, with the first two nearly grown, we had moved to Houston. After about two years there I was diagnosed with cancer, Hodgkin's. Many afternoons when the children came home from school they and some of their friends would sit on or beside my bed and we would visit. I enjoyed talking to them and hearing their ideas and comments. It was during a time my strength was low due to radiation treatments so I rested a lot. But it was a great treat to me to have the children sit and visit. I could know them; they knew someone would listen to them.

The sense of humor of your children will be demonstrated as they live and play together. Sometimes it is funny; sometimes it takes a little time to see the humor. Our boys would pull pranks on one another. The boys had a black and white paint horse named Pretty Boy. Very early one morning Paul along with a neighbor friend had gotten up early and gone out to the horse. It seemed I heard a nicker, sleepily I thought, "Oh, its just Pretty Boy", then, "wait I can not hear that horse from my bedroom!" About that time Todd woke up and called out "Mom, Pretty Boy is in my bedroom!" His brother and friend had led the horse up the back stairs, down the hall and into Todd's room to surprise him awake. The story was, in a way, funny later, not too much at the time, other than to Paul and his friend John.

Would your child do such an outlandish thing? You never know, children can be pretty innovative.

All too often the parent is attempting to instruct and raise children while keeping their head firmly planted in the sand. Danger signs go unnoticed and when crisis hits there is great shock. How did this happen? Little by little, step by step. Today is a confusing time to be a young person. Young people have been watching and considering the world around them. Obviously something is not quite right with the system running the world, and today's youth are aware there is a problem somewhere. Their world is full of pressure; peer pressure, scholastic pressure, pressure to succeed, pressure to meet parent

37

expectation. Any thinking person can see that the advice given and the examples shown to our youth are not producing the life they want to live. The old plan does not seem to be working. Our generation never faced either the challenges or the opportunities offered to today's youth. These young people may not be sure what plan will work, but they can see some new plan must be formulated. Young people today seem to know early on that a new way needs to be found. In a search for something new it is easy to be led into a wrong path. Some new influence in the life of a youth may become a guiding light. Remember, the same old adversary is still lurking about providing guidance in the wrong direction. Often the leader of a group your child wants to follow has the charisma and leadership to draw others. It ever has been true; the person with a dream, a vision, and excitement about that dream will draw others to the cause. Whatever the cause may be, followers are sure to get in line. Before you know it, here comes the leader person into the lives of confused, unsure youth. Could you say your children have seen the power of God and His hand on you enough to know it is by Him you are guided? You need to be sure you have helped build a firm foundation so the child has something to stand on for decision.

The list of things about which a young person is unsure is a long one. Many young people are not sure if someone, or if anyone loves them. Their body is ever changing and they aren't sure it is growing as they want it to, everything seems so awkward. Some kids wonder if they will ever fit their feet! They doubt they will ever have clear skin. Will they be accepted at school, at church, by peers? Can they just be themselves, and if so they wonder, who is myself anyway? It is important beyond words that your child knows he is loved and accepted. The importance of showing your love and assuring your child of your love and your acceptance can not be overstated. Let your children know you both, as parents love them, and also that God loves them. Rules and stipulations for behavior may be at times a source of argument, but really the child feels security at knowing you will keep them in those parameters of safety. When I was a teenager I remember feeling more secure knowing when my parents would curtail some things I might ask to do. It could be I did not know any way to get out of a situation other than to be able to say my parents would not allow me to do whatever it may have been.

Can your young people come comfortably to you to talk about their thoughts, the things on their heart? The subject may be a shock to you as a parent, but try not to show shock, just listen. You can be praying silently for wisdom as you listen! Is there a consistency and stability about your life that reassures those around you? Perhaps the friends of your children also need a listening ear. Their parents may not be available to them. Lifelong relationships are built as you visit with your children and their friends. In so few years they will be adults, will there be a foundation on which to build an adult friendship? It is paramount to a stable youth. Children can weather just about any of the storms teen life may blow their way, when they are confident they are loved and that Mom and Dad and their family will be there in case of trouble.

Problems will arise in life. The comforting thing to remember is God is bigger than any problem ever to arise. Give your children to God. Ask Him to keep them, to speak to them. Then tell the children you have given them to God. Let them know you love them but you do not have to worry about them. You, yourself, can never change anyone. Allow your heavenly Father to work in His way. It may be the Lord will use some other person to reach your child and be a guide. Thank your heavenly Father for the children God has given you. From the time a child is born the parent delights in watching his development. We love to tell of our child's accomplishments and talents and wonderful personality. Some parents, however, forget to let the child hear us say these good things. The child may only hear the correcting and the instructions. A little pat on the back goes a long way, a special treat, even a happy sticker now and then. Anything that singles out one particular child and lets the child know they are special to you. Everyone enjoys the good feeling from such action. It is easy to get too busy for this sort of thing. Allow God to be Lord over your child. Naturally this is easier said than done, just as it is not so simple to allow God to be Lord indeed over other areas of our life. Once you have given your child over to God, try not to heap stress upon yourself as the child struggles and makes a mistake here and there. It takes a lot of time and trying of ideas for a young person to develop their own personality and find out just who they are. Each child must decide for themselves whether or not to walk with God and live according to His Word. It may take some longer than others. Parents just keep praying.

The earlier a parent sets into action a plan to work with and through God's will, the earlier the parent will have some peace of mind and the sooner it becomes habit to see God the Father as a daily help. So often the wrong message has been transmitted to today's children, it has become difficult for them to find the right message. Have you ever dialed your phone, and clicked into another line? Strangers are talking and they can not hear you; it is confusing, who are these people, where did they come from? Just a crossed signal in the air. Children get confused by crossed signals. Perhaps if more children saw faith, or love, or peace; they would develop it in their own lives. There are times when a parent must show humility; be honest, and tell our children we have made mistakes; but here is what we found through those mistakes...Don't worry too much; your child already is aware you are not perfect! Try talking with the youth in way of comfortable conversation on a regular basis, rather than waiting until a troubling situation is underway. The time spent in talking and visiting with your child builds a friendship. Like any real friendship it takes cultivating, work, consistency, and genuine care and concern. If you have built a relationship of trust and friendship, when trouble does come your words will be much more influential. You may feel a note of repetition here, but the idea is worth a second mention. It took some time before Jim and I learned some of these things as parents, so we understand from more than one view point. It can be a great source of comfort to your children to know you are praying and to know that you are able to pray effectively for them.

41

Now that we are older and the children are grown it is a treat and blessing to just have coffee and visit with them. These are responsible young adults with intelligent input into the situations we discuss. They have input and advice worth considering and we enjoy talking with them. What an empty gap our life would have without such special times and conversations. It is amazing to us that with our many failings and ineptness, here stand such quality young adults. Certainly this is a work of grace.

Churches talk of the need for revival. How can anyone expect to have revival of any kind if we can not see revival within the home? God has always been interested in the day to day routine details of life. This is where our Christian walk is built and established. Perhaps mini revivals could be seen in home after home if the child of God could learn to give their family as well as their life over to the Father. The home and family is precious. It is imperative for the Christian to ask the Father to open our eyes, to teach us and show us fully just how precious the ties of family can be. Nothing else in this life after God and His will stands before the family as priority. With all of the curiosities and differences and challenges, and struggles, nothing else is quite like family. No one else knows us in quite the same way. Which could be why some people avoid the contact? No one else will be there for you in the way family will be there. God has given to my husband and me five children, very individual people. Each has their own ideas, strong attitudes, personality. We feel God gave us some great kids. Would we have wanted any of them to do some things differently? Oh yes, but it has to be their choice and we try to remember the journey is not yet over. Our children encourage us and help us and talk with us. They are each building their own lives now and most have a family. Which brings about one of life's great benefits - grandchildren! Now there is a treat from God. We are older now so we may not be with the grandchildren daily or train them as do their parents, but we will influence them. Remember that same old thought, yours is the only mind and the only heart you actually have the ability to change. However, by changing your mind and heart you never know how other people will be touched and changed. You may find it might be worthwhile to give it a try.

You never know how much your grandchildren watch you. I have an essay by Allora, our grand-daughter that is one of the most valued papers in my life. Her teacher asked the students to write a paper about a special person and Allora chose Grandma Leslie. It is first beautifully written, then very specific about the things she admired. This child in third grade took notice when gifts suited her tastes and interests and she could know both she and her brothers meant a lot to her grandfather and me. She mentioned areas of strength you might not realize a child would see. Make no mistake, children do not miss much. Perhaps some other mother or grandmother would be blessed by this little girl's thoughts and words, so I will include a copy of the paper at the end of this chapter.

Our Father loves us and loves our children, He wants to bless our homes if we will but give Him the opportunity. The power of God can hold back any of the troubles Satan can conjure up. God will get you through intact if you will stay in the Word of God and trust Him.

"And there is hope in thine end, saith the Lord, that thy children shall come again to their own border."

Next you will see Allora's essay, as she wrote it. To have your grandchild write such a thing is more than special and it is very humbling.

Allora Novak

"A Special Person" - My Grandma Leslie

My essay is about my Grandma Leslie. She is very special. She is great! She writes poems and stories and loves it when I write things. She loves God and sings and she helps the poor and other people. She makes our birthdays special by making us personal and learning, educational gifts.

Grandma Leslie lives in Texas. We can not see her that often. I think I got my writing skills from her. She is a beautiful writer because she writes songs, poems and stories that are from her heart.

She is a Christian who loves God. She sings in her choir at church and helps lots of people who need comfort. She is my Mom's mother and she is Scottish and Irish and had three sons and two daughters. Her and my Grandpa have a company that builds churches also.

Our birthdays and Christmas are always special because Grandma Leslie makes nice things and buys educational stuff for us. This Christmas she made me a canopy for my bed with flowers and lace and butterflies on it. I think she is a great person. She is talented in lots of things.

I wish we could see her more often but we can't because she is sick and has a cancer called Hodgkin's Lymphoma. She can't travel too well and she lives out in Houston, Texas. She is still special though because of all the things she does and the things she writes and also she loves us more than anything in the world!

PATIENCE ALONG THE HEAVENLY HIGHWAY

"Tribulation **worketh patience**, and patience, experience; and experience hope: and hope maketh not ashamed; because the love of God is shed abroad in our hearts by the Holy Ghost which is given unto us." Romans 5:3-5

"...nay, but by the law of faith." Romans 3:27 I "Ye are of God, little children, and have overcome them: because greater is he that is in you, than he that is in the world." John 4:4

Tribulation and trial, testing and struggles; trouble of every kind abound in our world. According to the message of the Scripture we just read we should have a land abounding in patient folk! Alas, such is not the case; in fact it is hard to find people who are patient. Surely God did not err when He directed Paul to write in Romans 5 "tribulation worketh patience". Man will sometimes replace "worketh" and insert "produces" or "makes" or even "forces". No drive through experience here, work and time is needed. Effort must be expended; the expected patience will not automatically descend upon us. Notice Paul wrote tribulation worketh patience. It is necessary to go through whatever the tribulation may be and complete the test. In today's society it is easy to fall into the habit of instant everything. God, our Father, however, changes not, He is still not instant. You do not drive through a window, nor do you click a mouse for Patience. Patience is, as it were, the reward for having passed the test of tribulation. Notice in Romans 3:27, "...nay, but by the law of faith." It is by this law of faith we shall overcome our tempter. (I John 4:4)

God's Word was not in error when stating tribulation worketh patience. In these pages I am using the King James Version of the Bible, hence "worketh". However it would be unlikely anyone can not understand the word is the same as works. Usually we can understand the words; it is just the trouble of accepting responsibility for them. It is man, not God who has failed whenever a scripture seems unfulfilled. Have you ever considered how futile and senseless it is that at a critical decision point in life, mortal failing man will question Almighty God? Do we as an adult heed when our four year old child argues and insists a thing be done other than what has been directed? Not if we want the child to grow with good training. The little child can not understand the situation; as we can not understand God's way or His purpose. When tribulation did not work patience, but rather developed anger, strife, depression, etc., in someone's life God is not to blame. Perhaps that person was not living in accordance with the law of faith. Life can be hard, and even overwhelming if one loses sight of God and His direction. The situation, the guidance, the help from above, all of the necessary elements were present to produce the patience, and experience, and hope. But those elements must be implemented according to plan. No one is forced by God to do as He directs, we have our own will, and it is our choice. Having accepted the grace to be saved and become a child of God He desires our fellowship and obedience; but He will not force His way into our heart. Until we invite the Holy Spirit to come in and dwell within our heart the wonderful blessings of God will be missing, yet the choice remains for each individual. Once you have let Him in your heart and life you can not imagine life without Him.

All of a sudden you become a new creature, your old man of sin is dead and the new man of Christ's spirit is raised. If you can just realize that you have only to listen to His guidance you can avoid a lot of trouble. So often we complicate God's plan for our lives. Until the will is given over to Christ and the heart is contrite, tribulation may bring more tribulation. But when we proceed through the tribulation then to experience to hope, we are in a blessed state indeed. Though hope is not the first step it is a great step, well worth reaching. Our Father takes us on a lifelong journey; leave out some of the steps and you miss some of the blessing and the teaching. When He saves you, you are saved, you are new inside, and you can live in confidence of a heavenly guide. Yet you do not know everything you need to know. Get into your Bible and begin to learn and to talk with the Lord. Today it is standard to find a shortcut in everything. We therefore think shortcuts will work with God as well. However, He changes not, remember, it is as it has ever been; best to follow God's direction, taking each step He shows you. We serve and follow a very precise and detailed Lord. Reading through the books of the Old Testament reveals how very detailed is our God. He was concerned about every aspect of life. His concern demonstrates His love for His children.

"The love of God is shed abroad in our hearts by the Holy Ghost which is given unto us." The love of God in your heart will be made apparent through kindness, a willingness to serve, a spirit of obedience toward Christ and His Word, and through love toward others, and also by a spirit of assurance. God's words are always true; these truths remain and work in today's society, the things of God never become obsolete. The child of God has but to obey the whole counsel of God. Doesn't that sound simple? In a way it is, but it may not be so easy. In trying to obey you have to learn to listen for God's direction. I have had God try to teach me and use such humble situations they could be missed. Not what I expected at all. My Father had to show me that if I gave something to another person feeling led by Him, I gave it as though it were to Him. The thing was no longer mine or my concern, no matter what the person did with the gift. God would know if I were sincere and following His will, and he would know if I were not. This was a difficult lesson for me. Sometimes another person will hurt you, or be uncaring. Just remember what you do is to Him and He always cares. Keep your faith fixed above.

Remember - faith; where is faith that God will hear and answer. Where is faith to save our children, faith to protect them? Where is the faith to see our needs met? How do we find it? As "faith cometh by hearing", listen for God's voice. In your heart where He lives He will speak to you, you can hear, through the heart not the ears, but clearly if you listen. He may speak through others, one on one or in a service. He has no limitations after all. When Jim and I were in Bible College one of the professors, Bro. Don Davis, would pray for his class that they would recall "those things they have learned". No study, no paying attention, there will not be much to recall. After hearing, do we listen and take these teachings into our daily lives? Or do we let them slip away unnoticed. The things of God, the reading, preaching and teaching of His word are paramount to having a victorious life. How else will we get to know this Friend that sticks closer than a brother?

The blessing and fulfillment, however, of living a victorious life is worth more than we can imagine. Sometimes in our life it seems everything is wrong, perhaps broke, or sick, no one seems to understand us, in school classes are too hard, our vehicle is not reliable or it is ugly, our neighbor is dreadful and wicked, our dog bit the kid down the street and his father is irate. One time our son's dog chased the neighbor's cat and unfortunately caught it on the cloth roof of his convertible, ruined the cat and the roof, the relationship, and his wallet. All sorts of things can be wrong but yet in our heart still rings a song, the joy is not gone. You learn to deal with life as it happens and go on. Such joy will bring strength and peace and the ability to

51

seek God's direction. There were some times when the children were still in our home and things were tight financially, I did not know if there was enough money for the groceries I needed. More than one time I have knelt beside the bed, laid out on the bed the twenty or thirty dollars I had to spend. Then I would give that to the Lord; tell Him I needed to fix meals for the family for that week. By the time I returned from the farmer's market and the grocery, somehow everything was provided! We always had good, filling, nutritious meals, plenty to share, and usually I had enough of the produce to stop and share some with a few of the women I had been visiting and witnessing to. How? I don't know other than that God performs "little" daily miracles in the lives of His children. Just have faith and obey Him.

Obedience to God and His Word will determine the level of peace and joy experienced, and certainly any power against the enemy. Hearts must be kept clean and open to the Father. Psalm 66:18 "if I regard iniquity in mine heart, he will not hear me." God never takes sin as lightly as we take it. Sin will be apparent to others just as the love of Christ is apparent when love abounds in our heart. Will you sin even after you have determined to follow Christ? Sure you will, just keep your account short; repent as soon as you see you're failing. It is not necessary that you sin on a regular basis and if you commune with your Father often that can grow less and less. Satan after all will continue to fire his darts at you. Really, the more you strive to serve Christ and walk with Him, the more you will be attacked. You have become a greater threat to Satan than the Christian doing nothing.

However, as you learn of Him, you learn how to hold up the shield of faith and use the various pieces of armor given the Christian for protection.

On this journey along the heavenly Highway life will bring many different situations, we will walk along with many different people, we will have many times of testing. On the job you may be unrewarded for extra work and effort, you may be misunderstood. Should this steal away your joy in Christ? No, Christ did not ignore you, man did; your reaction to the situation will show your character and Christianity. You are in a new family where you are accepted. The journey can be one of joyfulness and abundance. The Happy Goodmans used to sing a song called "Joy For The Journey". God will give you that, ask Him, expect it and act like you got it! If you do not, well then, the journey can be one of misery and depression, never quite getting hold of hope and victory. The choice is yours. God is Almighty, He can do anything, and He knows and loves you personally and cares very much about your daily life. You have the option of recognizing this wonderful fact and enjoying Him, or you may ignore it and be miserable and grouchy.

One day more than twenty years ago now I realized there was something physically wrong with me I could not ignore. We found out it was cancer, Hodgkin's stage II. It came at a time I thought was a high point along my walk with Christ. I felt so strong in Him and knew he could do anything. I was still young and strong and full of adventure for life. We were busy in our church and doing all the things "good church people" do. All of a sudden my life and the life of my family changed. I was thrown into a whole new culture at M.D. Anderson Cancer Center. What an overwhelming place, all sorts of people come there, all kinds of emotions are felt there, everything is serious, most things are confusing at first, every case can be fatal. For myself there was strong support from my church and friends and family. Many prayed for me and God gave me great grace and real peace. This did not make the trial easy by any means and the effects of this turn of events are still felt. But I noticed at the Center that attitudes make a huge difference. Those patients with strong wills to live, a positive outlook, some goal for which to reach, and real faith made better progress and recovery than did those who gave up or were negative. Even if you get the flu, if you go lay around and moan about how ill you are and how terrible you feel, you will be much sicker than if your attitude and spirit is good and you ask God what to do to improve your situation. Regular Bible reading of several chapters daily was already my practice so I knew if I asked Him God would show me a verse that could be "my verse" if you will for this trial. Now I suppose I did expect some uplifting, encouraging, even healing type of verse. God very clearly showed me Psalm 119:71, "It is good for me that I have been afflicted; that I might learn thy statutes." Surely this was the wrong verse! But He gave it again. And do you know He was right, through these years of one health challenge after another I have had to learn to trust His way, and use His strength. I am often amazed by what He can do with so little. He has made light shine in dark times and made hard roads gentle to walk. You have a lot of time to think and pray and consider where you are going when you have a serious illness. It is not possible to trust in your own strength, that may be gone, and you do not know if it will be returned. This is a good place to build in your soul an altar, place yourself upon it and give the sacrifice of acceptance with joy. You do not know who God will help through you; you may not even realize that His hand has become apparent upon your life.

Tribulation worketh, is a phrase that pushes people back in a cringe. Often however the work we see before us is not so bad as first thought, and the reward is more than worth the effort. Patience giving a quiet strong heart along with the hope which brings faith and joy is a wonderful reward.

How many more people might listen to the gospel, might seek to hear more of Christ, if they saw Him manifested in the lives of the "church people" as they say! In your heart, do you feel a greater number of people would be drawn to Christ if they could see real victory and holy power in the lives of Christians? You know it would! Hope maketh not ashamed, because the love of God is shed abroad in our hearts by the Holy Ghost which is given unto us. Christian, work and grow in order to know in your life there is never a reason to be ashamed of your testimony. Know in your heart of hearts that you are secure in your faith. Go ahead and exercise your faith. Don't just sit on the bench in the game of life, get into the action and be a real part of God's work.

How can our children learn to stand for right and stand against their peers, against great temptation and pressure to sin, when parents are teaching them there is no strength, no victory? Where will the children get their strength? Patience and hope do not fall from the sky upon us like a rain; tribulation worketh these. Before they get to "maketh not ashamed", our children and friends watching will learn that a life lived in and for Christ is a wonderful, strong and happy experience. Such a life is the only way those outside of Christ can know His Word is true for today, true for tomorrow, true for everyone who will come unto Him. The Christian has a huge responsibility, and a great opportunity to show the world that we have a wonderful Savior. Faith and joy in our Savior is enough to help make the world around us different and much better, person by person.

As we end this chapter, take a moment of your time to consider areas in your own life in which you feel God could be seen more clearly by others. Where are the areas in which you need more of God's help? Perhaps this will help you focus on being closer to the person your Father intended you would become in Him.

Consider for a moment:

Do your children know you have joy in Christ and faith in His Word?

Do your co-workers know Christ is all to you and you love Him?

Do your neighbors know yours is a house where they can find help and prayer?

Does your church know you are strong in the Word of God?

In your heart of hearts, do you know you are what God wants you to be?

Do you see miracles, special unusual things occur often in your life?

You can answer affirmatively to all of these questions. God wants you to be a beacon to shine out to others; He wants you to be happy and joyful in Him. Let Him give you the grace and mercy to live by faith and grow in hope.

A HAPPY HOME ON THE HEAVENLY HIGHWAY

A HAPPY HOME RECIPE

4 Cups of Love	2 Cups of loyalty
3 Cups of forgiveness	1 Cup of Friendship
2 spoons of Hope	2 spoons of Tenderness
4 Quarts of Faith	1 Barrel of Laughter

Take love and loyalty, mix it thoroughly with faith.

Blend it with tenderness, kindness, and understanding.

Add friendship and hope.

Sprinkle abundantly with laughter.

Bake it with sunshine.

Serve daily in generous helpings.

Together read I Corinthians 13:1-13 each week.

Insert your own name for "I" and "MY", etc.

Be sure that always on your table is found a

Good sized shaker of the salt of common sense,

And a jar of honey to sweeten a bitter day.

I Corinthians 13, "Though I speak with the tongue of men and of angels, and have not charity, I am become as sounding brass, or a tinkling cymbal. And though I have the gift of prophecy, and understand all mysteries, and all knowledge; and though I have all faith, so that I could remove mountains, and have not charity, I am nothing.

And though I bestow all my goods to feed the poor. And though I give my body to be burned, and have not charity, it profiteth me nothing. Charity suffereth long, and is kind; charity envieth not; charity vaunteth not itself, is not puffed up, doth not behave itself unseemly, seeketh not her own, is not easily provoked, thinketh no evil; rejoiceth not in iniquity, but rejoiceth in the truth; Beareth all things, believeth all things, hopeth all things, endureth all things.

Charity never faileth: but whether there be prophecies, they shall fail; whether there be tongues, they shall cease; whether there be knowledge, it shall vanish away, for we know in part, and we prophesy in part. But when that which is perfect is come, then that which is in part shall be done away. When I was a child, I spake as a child, I thought as a child: but when I became a man, I put away childish things.

For now we see through a glass darkly; but then face to face: now I know in part; but then shall I know even as also I am known. And now abideth faith, hope, charity, these three; but the greatest of these is charity."

Today in our uncertain world it is possible to have a happy home. The Word of God provides the recipe. As in any recipe the proper ingredients must first be assembled. Care should be taken to see all ingredients are of high quality and fresh, not stale and old. As the foundational ingredient in bread is a good flour, the foundation of the happy home is the sure knowledge of knowing Christ and knowing He is the base for all things. Your foundation will remain secure when it is Christ. As mentioned in an earlier chapter, Satan is the great deceiver, and he will try to fool you into thinking things will never work out for you, in fact it could be better if you and your spouse were not together. You probably are not compatible. Here's a little secret, you do not have to be compatible, just be companionable. Satan hates a happy home in Christ. Do not listen to him.

Satan will cause you to feel petty and be easily provoked causing strife, go right back to I Corinthians 13; run him out of your home. Don't be fooled by Satan's tactics. When troubles arise, look first for Satan to be at fault. Remember we talked earlier about sin being the key to all trouble. Sin must be confessed before God and forgiven by Him. Sin against God and His Word is always the core of any problem: God, His Word and His love is always the answer, even if it sounds too simple to be true. But the answer and solution is simple, not to be confused with "easy". Work and discipline and faith and perseverance are required here. Remember, confusion is of darkness, God will bring light and simplicity. In considering these things it will be easier to maintain the essential good humor toward life. Nothing helps keep a situation on a steady course better than a strong sense of humor. People take themselves very seriously. Learn to laugh at life, at yourself, and to openly enjoy others.

Look back at our Healthy Home Recipe. Have you been adding the right ingredients? Perhaps there has been too little of love? Or perhaps loyalty has been forgotten? How would a recipe for bread turn out if only half of the ingredients were used? Healthy meals and their preparation take a lot of time and thought. Today foods and goods are advertised as "natural", or "organically grown". Homemakers seek out the freshest, chemical free, or fat free foods to make the safest and tastiest dishes for a healthy family. Recipes are sought out that implement the newest trends toward health consciousness and carefully followed. All that caution and concern is good for you, but be careful not to neglect the very best, the most important in seeking the good. Don't leave out hope, and keep plenty of forgiveness on hand. In every family forgiveness is necessary again and again. As a parent your children will require your love and forgiveness over and over as they grow. In our family of five children someone was always playing a prank on another. It might be another of the children or it might be Mom or Dad. One incident stands out as memorable and certainly showing a case of loving the child "anyway"!

Our usual pattern was that I would take my husband's paycheck to the bank on Monday morning to deposit. This was over twenty years ago and I would go inside to the bank lobby. On one Sunday night our middle son thought it would be funny to startle me by dropping a frog into the snap pouch holding my identification cards. However I did not open my purse at home. It was not open until I stood in front of the teller in the bank lobby Monday morning. As the pouch was unsnapped, the frog leaped to his freedom straight at the startled teller! She threw her hands into the air, and screamed! I could have crawled under the floor, and could have strangled my son. Bank security guards rushed over to the commotion with hands on their guns. "Frog!" The girl exclaimed. "Frog"? The guard asked. "Yes, a frog jumped from her purse right onto me." said the girl. The guards wanted to know if I had given her a note about a robbery or money, if I had said anything. On deciding that only the frog had been loosed, I was detained as the bank was searched to find the actual robber since by now it was felt I could be the distraction. After what seemed forever, no offender had been found. I was escorted by a guard to my car. Having been humiliated in front of the entire bank I crept away, shaking and embarrassed. It was obvious to me this was the doing of Todd. Later while relating this tale of great woe to the family at home, there was raucous laughter. They thought it was the funniest thing they ever heard. Now you can imagine it took some measure of forgiveness to love this son at just that moment! But today Todd has children, so who knows what he may learn! We did of course change to another bank for business. Also no one tried to pull the same prank again!

Positive results are assured upon following God's plan for a happy home. His Word never fails, never changes, and is ever true. The more often you work on this recipe the stronger and wiser you will become. The more a sense of humor is in place the more strife is diluted. The more love and forgiveness is exhibited the less room there is for argument and conflict. As a family of happiness and love and strength, you will have happiness and hope to share with other homes. There are a lot of homes, and children from those homes that never get enough of happiness and hope, never experience a happy home.

Among your circle of friends has anyone ever given out to the group containers of starter for friendship cake? It is a favorite recipe to give out to a group; it grows and grows a never ending supply. The happy home recipe also is a great recipe to spread around, and can be expanded in unlimited supply. There is no end to God's love, or His love in us. So go ahead, get out a big bowl for the Word, and get a long spoon of good sense and begin to mix up your own happy home recipe.

THE WOMAN ON THE HEAVENLY HIGHWAY

There is a "Recipe for Charm" about an old Quaker woman. She was distinguished for her youthful appearance and was asked what she used to preserve her charms. She replied sweetly; "I use for the lips, truth; for the voice, prayer; for the eyes, pity; for the hands, charity; for the figure, uprightness; and for the heart, love."

The charms developed by this Quaker lady will enhance any woman. These are the things that make the beauty of Christ remain a deep well in a woman and allow her to have the living water to refresh others. These are the charms the Proverbs woman had developed. We women spend much time on our physical appearance, our make-up, or clothes, or figure; and yet we too often neglect the most important things. Nothing outward will have a lasting beauty without the character, and truth and strength given to us in the Word of God. What you put in your heart and in your mind will affect your life and even your look, just as what you eat affects your look. If we are careful to tend to these mortal bodies, feed them, clean them, and pet them; should we not be careful to tend the immortal soul? The more of the character of Christ, of the Word of God we can adapt to our own life, the more we will have a strong, lasting presence among men.

Proverbs 31:10, "Who can find a virtuous woman? For her price is far above rubies". This woman would not have much time for idle gossip or lying around. She is out in the markets buying and selling, buying fields, taking care of her household, making clothes, helping others in need, she is a good business woman, she makes her husband proud and she is proud of him; he trusts her. If everything listed in this chapter as being done by this virtuous woman were entered into a day planner it would be a heavy schedule. How well could you organize your schedule to include the business she conducted, the sewing, the cooking, and the taking care of her household? This woman took time to plan what she had to do, thought about it, prayed about it, and put real effort into doing all she could to keep her world in order. The tasks accomplished by the Proverbs 31 woman took forethought and real planning, these things could not just accidentally happen. Knowing her family was well clothed and fed she reached out to the poor. She conducted herself wisely in the market place and in business, for this was no shrinking violet lady. Her heart was kind to help others. This is an admirable woman.

Throughout the Scriptures are illustrations of people and how they lived their lives. What kind of work they did, how charitable they were, or how hard their heart was. Do you ever think as you read these passages what would be said if it were **you** being described? Would God have to leave out the acts of kindness, or the strength and honor shown by the person? Could it be said of you that you speak with wisdom? Do your children rise up and call you blessed? Do you feel inside that you are all God wants you to be? What is it that He would want anyway? Does He want more than church attendance? Oh yes He does! Does He want more than being polite to people! Oh yes He does. Our Savior lived among men as our example. These illustrations left us in His Word are for examples and instruction. The woman read of here is not the only woman to live this way; to keep her home and life in order, to care for others, to be diligent and hard working. God intended women to continue to use this as example and to try to implement these things into their own life.

There will be a time that each of us will meet God and leave this life. We all will leave something behind with those that knew us. What do people think of when they think of you? What could be written of you? Could it be said of you as it was of this lady in Proverbs, that you are a virtuous woman, an industrious woman? Or as of the old Quaker woman that you are full of grace and kind hearted? God help us that we might be concerned about these most important inner things in our lives. No wonder the Word of God remarked on the rarity of this woman by stating, "Her price is far above rubies."

PRAYERS IN THE AIR

Listen, can you hear it moving through the trees?

The rustling sound of a soft gentle breeze.

Tis the end of a wearisome long hot day.

It seems that some one has stopped to pray.

Their earnest prayer is rising high,

On to the Father beyond the sky.

Now rising heavenward that heart felt prayer;

Moves like a melody in the air.

And if you're quiet, you just be still,

God will your heart with promise fill.

Then on another, better day,

Twill be your time to kneel and pray.

When other weary saints will feel the breeze;

As a heavenward prayer moves through the trees.

(LMJ)

WHERE IS GOD IN YOUR LIFE ALONG THE HEAVENLY HIGHWAY?

"When thou goest, it shall lead thee, when thou sleepest, it shall keep thee, and when thou awakest, it shall talk with thee." Proverbs 6:22

What a blessed comforting promise these words offer the reader. Whether walking through the business of the day, or when night comes for sleep, then at the dawn of a new day, He is there. In your life, is God right there? Is He close enough for you to converse often with Him, or must you seek and wait to find Him? What is He to you? God your Father wants to be the center of your life, He wants you to have the abundant full life spoken of in His Word. Have you given Him the place of dwelling in your heart so that He can be the very center of your life?

To the vast majority of people Jesus Christ is not the center of their life. Far too many people are themselves the center of their life and they protect that point avidly. God did say "few there be that find it" in speaking of the straight and narrow way. Thanks be we can always ask Him into our heart if we have not done so. To some people God could be portrayed by the life preserver hanging on a ship's rail in case of emergency. His being is accepted, even the fact that He is important - to a degree but not for everyday or for serious consideration. There are some churches with members claiming to know and love God but you find they most love argument and debate about God. Would our Father have left us the wonderful Book of Books and kept it all this long time for it to be a mind game, a challenge for one another? Christ said He held His Word above His Name; He admonished believers to understand the Word was eternal. It is also to be read and heeded in our day to day life. We have great liberty once Christ has come to dwell within our heart. Our joy is unspeakable, our peace is beyond understanding, and our strength is great through Him that is mighty. We often act and live as though we have no idea of the power and happiness and grace now within our own heart.

My home is in Houston, Texas, I have always lived in the United States of America. It is easy here to take our liberty as citizens of a free country for granted. It is all we have known. For us there is no fear of danger should we make a commitment to live for Christ. There may be some adjustment in our personal life, but we do not fear persecution or danger for being Christian. In many countries this is not the case, as we are seeing more and more as terrorism and wars spread. Sadly many of the battles are fought in the name of one or another religion. In the name of their god people take other lives, ruin cities, destroy cultures, commit horrible acts upon one another. In such places the cost is very dear to openly claim to serve Christ. Daily life and its ever present danger draws these Christians close to their Savior's side for comfort. To them prayer is as dear as food, to have even a scrap of the Word of God is dear and precious. We do not even realize how blessed we are to be free.

The love of God reaches to all men in every condition. The word of God is intended to comfort and guide men and women worldwide. He would that all men be saved. Would you feel a pang of guilt if examples of your life were given to describe to someone how to live for Christ? Well, even if this is so, you have hope. His love can pull you from a soft cushion of comfort and ease just as well as He pulls men from great peril. Provision has already been made for you to have a place of peace and rest and security and hope. You may feel a knocking at your heart's door. Open it and Christ will enter your heart and life. He will make your life worthwhile and wonderful.

People the world over seek relief from stress, confusion, and the daily pressures of their life. They look on every avenue. Bars are full of people trying to forget something, or getting help to be strong. Mountains of books offer instruction to find the answer to life's need. Seminars are conducted to lead us into some new truth. New religions are founded to build the mind and soul. There is every kind of self help and new image help out there. Huge sums of money are spent to reach the right plateau. Power speakers charge your adrenaline to make you an overcomer in adversity. Fitness experts work the body to overcome anything and keep the mind from pulling you down. People work so hard at being peaceful and happy they have created just another great stress for themselves. Satan loves to see people caught up in all of these things. There is no time for God and no place for Him in a lot of the loves on this whirling treadmill. Go ahead, he urges, give it all - for anything but God Almighty and His Word.

Give yourself the chance to actually know the joy and peace you seek, by looking to God and His Word for the right answers. Here is your foundation. Once you have accepted the gift of life through the blood of Jesus Christ, the Holy Spirit of Christ moves in to stay in the new heart. Old things are passed way and you are made new. There is an undeniable touch of God when He comes into your heart. For a few nights try reading Proverbs 6:22 aloud before you go to sleep. Calmness will settle in your mind. During the business day you may even find your mind is able to function with greater clarity as you work and make decisions. You have assured yourself that God, very God, will keep you and will be with you. What a great realization! In your newness as a Christian you should feel a hunger for His Word, the more you take of it the more you will desire. His Word becomes precious food for your soul, and you will be satisfied and complete. "It shall talk with thee". With Proverbs 6:22 as your daily walk there will be close fellowship with the Lord. How could you feel alone when you are so close to He Who said, "I will never leave thee nor forsake thee"? Christ will be with you, and you will know He is with you.

On your daily journey, is Christ the light that shines to show the way? "When thou goest, it shall lead thee". Believe these words; take joy and strength in them. Knowing God will lead you, and keeping close fellowship with Him your path is made secure and sure. Never would a question arise as to where God is in our life, because you keep close by Him. God is just where He wants to be, at the center of your life.

In your heart rings a song of victory and joy when Jesus Christ is the song you sing. The song will radiate from you as a warm glow touching others. No one sings like the child of God. Hearts full of God's Word and His love are happy, peaceful singing hearts. The world knows many kinds of music, great talent, great voices, but none able to touch a heart in the way of the songs of faith. Such music has a depth no other music can match. The child of God sings of eternal foundational truths.

Where is God in your life? In the everyday fabric of life how wide is God's influence? Does His will influence the scheduling of your calendar? If Sunday and probably only a little piece of that day is the only time you give the Lord, you are missing a great deal. When it takes a crisis for you to call upon God, you have missed the best He has for you. God intends for His children to live in blessing and joy here, in this life. The words left in the Bible are to direct us on the journey along the Heavenly Highway as we live for Him; now, not in a far off sometime.

Walk close beside the Savior, be blessed by His presence. When you hear the Word preached or taught, take it for your life guide; use

75

the words in your life. These are words for our instruction to help in daily life. Use the messages for encouragement, for instruction to reach out and draw someone else along the path you have found. Eye hath not seen nor ear heard what God hath prepared. We can not even imagine what God will do. But He knows, and if you talk with God often, He will tell you more and more as you become open to hear Him. What a superb method of eliminating stress from your life!

One of the easiest subjects about which to make jokes is stress in daily life. So many people relate to the subject. It has become so overwhelming and is accepted as a part of normal existence that we must look at stress through a filter of humor just to deal with so many issues. Never has there been a time, or so it seems, when so many people had so little peace. God has been pushed out of so many areas of life there is a great cold vacuum left. Getting a good night's sleep is difficult for so many people, insomnia is a common malady. "When thou sleepest, it shall keep thee" is of huge importance. Nerves are unsteady in today's world; a peaceful mind is but a pipedream. Did you know that the two most prescribed drugs today are Prozac and Prilosec? Supposedly these medications are intended to help stabilize the mind and digestive system. In truth the medications may be dangerous. However the need is great, people have to find relief. Every imaginable kind of stress relief is marketed from aroma candles and oils to mood altering music to natural herbs, along with the old standbys of drink and drugs. Peace with God would do so much more and with no harm to your body, as well as having capability to last a lifetime and longer. Since we will live for eternity that is good news.

Sometimes God's children seem to forget the reality that Christ will keep His child and give great peace. There is a rest in God to be had today in your life. It is a simple thing to talk with God, to fellowship with Him; after all, He said He would be closer than a brother. Sometimes a simple truth is hard for people to accept. We love to complicate things. After all of the books we have read and the seminars we have attended so much knowledge is stored in our minds simple truths may seem beneath our level. People want to do something very religious or important; in so doing everything becomes complicated. Flesh has overtaken the spirit again, creating age old problems. Simple uncontrived truths are often the hardest ones to deal with and to accept as fact. Do yourself a favor, go ahead and accept the Word of God as truth.

Some years ago we heard an old country preacher from a remote area of the hills of North Carolina. For many years he had driven or walked through woods and to camps and logging outfits, remote homes, concrete plants, taking God's Word to people. Between times of preaching while standing on a cut stump of a tree the old man took time to read his Bible, then to quietly think through what he had read. He had a plain, nearly childlike manner of talking to the Lord with a complete acceptance of God's presence and His will for him. During one of his messages he remarked in answer to questions about knowing so much of God.

"Well, I don't know but a couple of things for sure. One of them is I know there is God. And another thing is I ain't Him. The last thing I know for sure is that God, not me, is always right!" Now this old preacher had led what would appear to the average person to be a hard life. He never knew many of the comforts or luxuries of this world. Yet he never thought he had a hard time. He always knew how to find and talk to God. His place was secure, his faith sound, his joy unfettered, his peace untainted. No one needed to counsel this man or give him medication or help him find himself. Without knowing it this man has great treasure in his life. Find in your heart and mind a way to drop yourself into the able hands of the Savior, those hands that created the entire universe. He will keep you.

Look again at the blessed promise in the verse we have been considering. If God is not where He wants to be in your life, how can you ever hope to be where you want to be in your life? There are so many blessings, so many adventures your heavenly Father has for you. Utilize the helpful, hopeful words of Proverbs 6:22 every day of your life and you will not wonder where you are or where God is in your life. Blessed assurance will fill your soul and joy will be your song.

HOLD ON FOR THE VICTORY

"When thou goest, it shall lead thee;

When thou sleepest, it shall keep thee;

When thou wakest, it shall talk with thee."

And He says to hold on for the victory.

Through all the ages, God gave a guide.

He left His Word in a book that will abide.

The path for His children may be stony and long.

But within their heart His Word keeps a song.

You may feel lonely, see dark all around,

You listen for hope, but don't hear a sound.

Then deep down inside a tiny light gleams,

And you say, I'm alright, for I know I'm redeemed!

When thou goest, it shall lead thee;

When thou sleepest, it shall keep thee;

When thou wakest, it shall talk with thee.

And He says to hold on for the victory.

(LMJ)

THE GOOD MIND ALONG THE HEAVENLY HIGHWAY

"Let this mind be in you, which was also in Christ Jesus:"
Philippians 2:5

What a wonderful thought that we could indeed have within us a mind like Christ Jesus! Think quickly, how often in the last few days have you heard someone use the phrase, "I'm sorry, I guess I just forgot?" People often forget things, things they do know, but that somehow are hidden for the moment in the jumble of facts and data in the mind. Have you ever, for instance, put eggs to boil on the stove, then gotten busy with something else until you smelled something unpleasant? Or perhaps dashed out of the house in a hurry to an engagement, not remembering an earlier thought to yourself to put gas in your vehicle? We all forget things. The human mind is a complicated mysterious thing. At times it appears the mind is playing tricks. For instance, in the middle of a serious discussion some silly foolish thought pops into the mind like a toy jack-in-the-box, bringing an inappropriate temptation to laugh. Another time, when in earnest prayer, ungodly or impure thoughts creep into the mind. A shudder comes over as guilt for such weakness engulfs the stricken mind. No one is alone in having these uncomfortable moments. We have an adversary not to be forgotten, one who is ever ready to distract the mind, or disrupt life any way possible. He is the author of confusion and destroys peace at every opportunity. Human minds are a favorite playground for Satan. But, though there is a formidable foe, yet there is help in God's Word from One Who can always overcome Satan and his wiles.

Philippians 4:8 & 9, "Finally, brethren, whatsoever things are true, whatsoever things are honest, whatsoever things are just, whatsoever things are pure, whatsoever things are of good report; if there be any virtue, and if there be any praise, think on these things. Those things, which ye have both learned, and received, and heard, and seen in me, do: and the God of peace shall be with you."

"And the God of peace shall be with you." What a comforting, encouraging promise. Be very sure, of course, that you get to the promise by way of the preceding conditions. "Think on these things", this is your responsibility. Where is your mind? Where does it go in troublesome hours? Do you seek God and His help, quiet your mind and steady it with scripture, or do you take a medication to forget and obscure the situation? How often do we remember those things we have both learned, and received, and heard, and seen in Christ? The more of God and His Word in our mind, the less room is available for Satan's wiles.

Walking through a book store will clearly indicate the great preoccupation with man and his mind. People from every walk of life and culture seek books and tapes to help their mind, make them better, and make them more of whatever it is they seek; help to change their life. Authors can sell just about any book claiming to easily improve the mind. "Just follow this simple pattern", "Ten easy steps to a better life" the author will claim. Loaded shelves hold books to improve, deepen, clear, educate further the mind; add success, add positive, be healthier, or add spiritual thoughts. All of these categories do not include the books to entertain the mind, this list is endless. It can be extremely confusing to determine which books are worthwhile for you. Most people see the advantage of ongoing education. Every Christian knows in his heart the necessity to continue to learn more of Christ and the Word of God. However, finding the material best for you can be confusing with so many choices, since such a diversity of need exists in life. Ask your pastor or someone you know to be secure and knowledgeable concerning the things of God. Your church may have a library you can access. First and foremost will be the Word of God. Nothing else can compare to your Bible, though other works may help you in application and understanding of using God's Word in your daily life. Strong's Concordance is a greatly useful tool for Bible study. Most Christian bookstores will have the book. Another handy basic book is the Haley's Bible Handbook, which holds a wealth of information in a small book. You might keep a notebook listing names of authors, publishers, book titles. In a while you will see a direction God is guiding your study and development. You will learn how and where to find information addressing the areas of interest to you. Biographies are a great way to learn how God has used different people in many fields. These books help you see the way God helps His children in unusual situations, you are able to know of miracles in the lives of Christians in times when nothing but God would suffice. No Christian grows strong or grows to the place God would have him serve without taking the time to read. Without argument the first, the most important and best book to read is your Bible, it is God's Word to you, His child. In the pages of the Bible are found all we need for life. People today are too busy, too tired, life pulls in every direction, life is filled with too much stress. Reading will help to develop the discipline necessary to live a strong Christian life. Remember however these are helpful tools to use for the new mind God has put in you when you were born anew in Him. Trust first and foremost the guidance of the Holy Ghost of God in you. Now once again read Philippians 4:8 & 9.

"...whatsoever things are...
just...pure...lovely...of good report...if there be virtue...
if there be any praise...think on these.
Those things which ye have...
both learned...and received...and heard...and seen in me...
and the God of peace shall be with you."

Imagine what it could do to your mind were you to keep your thoughts within this strong framework. Why, you would feel so strong and positive and happy in the Lord you would probably be dangerous! Suppose you put this theory to the test, as it were, and try fitting thoughts, words spoken, movies or television watched, music, tapes, the conversations you hear, all into the pattern God gave. What do you think? How accurately do the words "just, pure, lovely, good report, virtue, praise" describe what you see? The idea gives a sobering thought does it not? Should the answer not be all you would wish, take heart; God is always there to be our guide and help.

A masters degree in theology is not needed to understand verse 9..."Do: and the God of peace shall be with you." Do you wonder if the opposite may also be true - don't do and the God of peace will not be with you? Many Christians hope not, because all too often people fall very short of the high demands found in God's Word. It may be a good thing to read improving books, but do remember to use the Book of Books for foundational truth. Whatever else you read must be in harmony with the Bible. Allow God in your life to help in choosing books. God will have liberty to be a guide when enough time is spent communing with Him through prayer and in His Word. In the soul of God's children dwells the Holy Spirit. He is ever with us. The Holy Spirit was given for a comfort and a guide and to provide the power to overcome Satan's attacks. Satan will try to fool you into thinking the Bible is too complicated, too difficult, too deep, hard language, totally outdated. Nothing could be further from the truth. The Holy Spirit of

85

God, living in your innermost being, will help you to understand what you need to know. You just have to remain on speaking terms with Him. As has been said, Satan is ever the great deceiver. Notice the pure simplicity of these verses as read carefully, word by word. Our Father would never have given a Book He would protect for all time, honor above all else and insist all of His children read it and be familiar with it unless He intended they could use the book! God would never have commanded the Words be read daily, in homes, in all places, had it not been intended the reader would comprehend and follow His words.

In the Gospels as Jesus talked with people He always related to whatever their state in life might be. To the shepherd, He spoke of sheep, wolves, and goats; to the husbandmen of vineyards, trees, growing, always subjects people easily understood. Try to keep in mind that there is always a basic practicality in the Scripture. It is never difficult to learn the "shop talk" of your profession; be it teaching, mechanics, or construction, medical, computer related, real estate, banking, or any other field of work. Whatever the job is you learn to "talk the talk" of the thing. Why then should it be difficult to learn how God talks? He is after all the heavenly Father to whom we may freely go at any time. How can His children know what to say in prayer? I would like to be able to speak Spanish, it is a beautiful language. I know a little and make attempts to learn, have a disk to study and practice on a willing friend here and there. But I do not work at it as a true student. When we go to Mexico or some other place where Spanish is spoken I feel more comfortable trying, that is all I hear around me and I can not communicate with the people if I do not try their language. It begins to seem natural and the words make sense.

By getting to know our Father intimately, we learn to speak with, and understand the voice of God Almighty. The more time you spend in prayer, Bible reading, and communion with your Father the more precious the time becomes as your ability to converse with Him grows. There is nothing this side of heaven to equal that moment when you have emptied your heart to God, prayed through some scriptures with Him, waited on Him until, blessed moment! You know the overflowing warmth of His love and touch embrace and engulf you. Just as you are never the same after you have repented and received Christ as your Savior, and He has moved into your innermost heart; so you are never the same anytime He touches your life, your heart. Did you know God Almighty wants you to walk every day, in your ordinary life, with His hand upon you? What an astounding thought that God wants to be so near us, and how comforting to know He will stay that near to us if we but bid Him.

"If there be any virtue, and if there be any praise, think on these things."

Are there areas in your life you need God's help to gain control of your mind?

Following are some scriptures to encourage you. Take a little time and honestly look at your attitude toward God and His Word. Sometimes it is good to set new goals for our spiritual life as much as we do in our business life. Here's an exercise to try.

AVERAGE TIME SPENT:

In prayer _____

In reading God's Word_____

Praising God and singing in your home or wherever you are_____

Sharing with someone about the Word_____

Finding new worthwhile books to read_____

Setting life goals_____

Setting spiritual goals_____

Reading frivolous material_____

Watching worthwhile viewings_____

Watching frivolous viewings_____

Gossiping with friends_____

In unnecessary shopping_____

In helping others_____

In letting family know they are loved_____

In being an encouragement to others_____

This list makes you think doesn't it?

The following Scriptures will help strengthen your mind.

Matthew 22:37

Luke 12:29

Philippians 2:5; 4:8,9

II Timothy 1:7

Isaiah 26:3

Mark 5:15

Romans 7:25; 8:6; 12:2

II Thessalonians 2:2

Leviticus 24:12

Lamentations 3:21

Let Christ keep your mind and strengthen it and you will not have to worry about losing it. "Let this mind be in you, which was also in Christ Jesus:" Philippians 2:5

STABLILITY ALONG THE HEAVENLY HIGHWAY

Isaiah 55:8&9, "For my thoughts are not your thoughts, neither are your ways my ways, saith the Lord. For as the heavens are higher than the earth, so are my ways higher than your ways, and my thoughts than your thoughts."

Philippians 4:7, "And the peace of God, which passeth all understanding, shall keep your hearts and minds through Christ Jesus."

Blessed promise to have peace beyond understanding in any situation. Troublesome times occur in every life at one time or another. In the midst of the troubling storms your stability in Christ may appear to be threatened. The weight of feeling under attack becomes oppressive. Satan, that old attacker can come at us from any direction. The attack may come to weary one with health challenges;

it may cause the squeeze of financial needs; perhaps the attack will be dealing with emotional stress through the work place; or an attack of stress and trouble in the home. He always knows where to find the spot of weak flesh. Sometimes he may attack from many areas at once.

In our home there was a time in our life when it felt everything was falling all at once. My husband, Jim and I had always been strong, hard workers. We were very involved with our church, the children were doing well. Then I noticed some symptoms and was diagnosed with cancer, Hodgkin's stage II, also one of our children took a course of going through a time of great challenge and hurt in her life. We had four more children in the house to care for, the youngest only three years old. Not long after the diagnosis and the wearisome long battery of testing, then surgery, all those things, came yet a further blow. Jim worked with a man we considered a friend in a business at which he was very good, had had a particularly good year. One morning during all of these other trials while the owner, the friend, was away, Jim was met with the news that he was being terminated! This was not the blessing we expected! But through all of these things God gave great grace. We worked and prayed and God blessed in each of the areas of trouble. God is always able to keep His children. The grace of God kept us from fear of the cancer and anger at the illness, which left me strength to survive. He is a good God and can walk with you through any valley. Was it easy? Not most days. But brothers and sisters in Christ helped us through, they prayed, they helped with the kids. Our family was there, and the kids learned to do a lot of things when it was needed. We just have to remember what His Word has told us.

Grab a tight hold to God's Word and stand on it. Too often the child of God spends what little strength he has left after his struggles trying to "figure out" God. Save your energy, you need it! Our Father can do His part if man will do the part set out for man. God has already said His thoughts are not our thoughts; that His peace passes understanding. If that peace passes understanding, you probably will not be able to understand it! We knew an old country preacher who would say "If you can figure a thing out and understand it, it can't be God, 'cause He is beyond our understanding"! Just accept Christ at His Word; His way, His peace; and let Him keep you. Certainly He is able.

One of the names used to describe those in Christ is Believer, we are Believers. Yet do we actually believe? Does it show in your life that you believe? The more we believe of what He has already told us, the more joy, peace, help and direction will be ours. Sounds simple doesn't it? If you have not made it a point to allow God to guide you without question, you will find it a most fulfilling situation on making this decision. How often do you hear people question why God does one thing or another? They are searching for God's reason in every trial. Relax! Don't question His voice as He speaks to you, just listen and heed the word. He already said we can not understand. It is not necessary to understand; it is, however, necessary to be willing to know what the Lord wants us to do now, and where He wants us to go at this present time. Search for your answers in the

Word of God, know His Word. The acceptance of God's Word and His will is the instrument through which will be found true peace.

When a major part of a person's energy is spent in seeking reasons for God's working, or reasons for life's happenings, soon that person will have no energy left for anything productive. I have known people it seems have a "worry committee" and they can find every speck of disaster that could happen, long before it actually does. Remember the story of Chicken Little and "the sky is falling"? Well, the sky was not and did not fall. Be careful, depression can set in with its brooding dark cloud, confusion will cloud the mind. As Christians we can know without doubt our Father is in charge, there need be no fear. The light of Christ's love will roll away a dark cloud. When we take our Father's hand, confusion drops by the wayside as we remember; He always knows the way. I don't know about you but this is great news for me. One of my doctors has told me I am "directionally challenged"! It seems I am never sure which way to go. I get there but may have my own special route. Knowledge and the freedom from fear relieve stress, making it possible for the Lord to work through the heart and life of the Christian. With this realization in the life of a Christian, energy is available for a stormy situation; to meet the need and take care of it. Grace relieved the fear so your mind can now be fixed on Christ. "Let this mind be in you as was also in Christ Jesus."

Certainly there is no question this world needs so very much help; things are in a mess. A true love of God puts in the heart of the Christian the desire to help somehow, to want to make a difference for those in need of the Savior. One of the best things God's children can do toward making a difference is to give the world solid, secure, directed, stable Christians. Such people will stand out like a beacon in a lighthouse. Other people are drawn to someone with a stability and peace about them. Stability is becoming more and more rare. People need to notice stability in the Christian; it will draw the lost to Christ. Most certainly today's youth need an example of stability. They have not seen enough so far to assure them. We want to see more people come to a life changing knowledge of Christ. By God's Word and His grace the child of God has access to all the stability he could need.

Recognizing then, such need, and the answer to the need, may we take time to pray, asking our great God and Father to give us something to make a change in the lives of the people we touch. Wonderful that so high and holy a God would care so very much for such creatures as we are and love us as only God Almighty can love. And the peace of God shall keep your hearts and minds through Christ Jesus. In the book of Joshua 14:8 & 9 & 12 the story is written of a man who personifies stability over a long period. I love the story of Caleb and his mountain. Few men stood as did Caleb the way he waited for his mountain. Consider with me these things about this great stalwart soldier of Christ.

You do not take, do not conquer the mountain until you have come through many campaigns; won, and lost many battles. During all of those battles he knew God was with him and that God's promise would be secure. Caleb took his mountain. Not in the fire of his youth but in his later years. After many years of being faithful, of battling the enemy, Caleb had a firm determination that through Jehovah God he would conquer his mountain. Soldier hard body held proud and erect he marched ahead. Fiercely determined in the assurance that he marched neath the banner of God Almighty, he was unshakeable. Caleb felt the surety born of having God's promise. Forty five years earlier he had told Moses, "Nevertheless my brethren that went up with me made the heart of the people melt: but I wholly followed the Lord my God. And Moses sware on that day, saying, Surely the land whereon thy feet have trodden shall be thine inheritance and thy children's forever, because thou hast wholly followed the Lord thy God"

Sword held firmly in a strong sure hand he directed his men onward. I want that mountain it belongs to me. (see verse 14:12).

Do you have a mountain you want? Is there a deep desire burning in your soul? Daily obedience to God and His Word will bring you ever nearer your mountain. Month after month, year after year of being where God wants you and what God wants you to be are the path to your mountain. The battles you endure each teach you a little more of what you'll need for your mountain. The victories won add incentive to continue steadfast in the faith wherewith we are called. Even the inevitable losses teach us and help to build us up. Along the way we grow stronger in the knowledge of the Word that dwells within our heart.

The world seems overwhelmingly filled with confusion. And so it is. Yet the Christian, rightly tuned to Christ continues steadfastly on, whatever may come. The promise, "there remaineth therefore a rest unto the children of God", whispers sweet peace to the soul. Caleb knew whom he served, he knew what was expected of him, and he knew what his inheritance was. He was willing to war, to work, to wait many years to gain that inheritance.

Sometimes we will sing a song like Bill Harvey's "I Want That Mountain", and try to have faith to reach and attain our own mountain - immediately. But the great mountains of our lives are not taken in a moment. They are not taken lightly. God wants us to be prepared when we get to the mountain. There are victories to be won daily, hills we can peak in the infancy of our Christian walk. But it may be that we might not even know what our great mountain is until we have walked a time with the Savior. The greatly respected missionary, Adoniram Judson's initial objective was not even Burma. But his mark for Christ upon Burma remains indelible. His years of service were many and long. His hardships were great; seemingly his reward for exhausting labor was very small indeed. But the entire world looks at this man as a testimony, an encouragement to stay at your work, in your place, in God's will; that He may interweave your service and your life into His great master plan for man and time.

Caleb said, "I wholly followed the Lord my God." Then in verse 12, "Now therefore give me this mountain." His first statement being honest, he could in confidence make the second. No frivolity about this man's life. His faith was not purchased for fifty dollars at a seminar. It was not a method of thinking positively in a frenzied climate where the adrenaline and emotion runs high. Nor may our faith be so if we are to attain that peak Christ has for each of us. The emotional kind of "faith" springs up quickly; grows gaudy, big and bright, like the sunflower, then finds its season soon over; and its impact very small. No, child of God, we are to grow more like the oak tree. Constantly progressing, growing ever more solid, tall and sure; ever more valuable; solid and serene standing tall above the wildly painted sunflower; we offer to all who come near a sense of rest and good and stability.

Now therefore give me this mountain. Not spoken as a teasing child begging a favor, but as the heart's desire of a mature Christian. We may not know exactly what our mountain is at this point of the journey. But as we pray and read God's Word and commune with Him, He will show a glimmer in the corner of our mind; a vision as it was, of what He has for us. To others, perhaps even to us, it may seem a very insignificant hill indeed. Yet we do not measure things the same way as our Lord. We can not see His final purpose. Therefore we are to walk on, as did Caleb, sometimes alone or with only one other; walk on in the path God shows us. Walk in praise, walk in peace, and walk in the assurance you never walk alone. Fight the battles, rejoice in the victories, repent over the losses, but go on in order that God may grant you therefore the mountain - because thou hast wholly followed the Lord thy God.

ABOUT THE AUTHOR

Life experience and God's many blessings, as well as her five children, have given the author a wealth of material from which to draw for the book. She has worked in several areas of ministry and met an interesting variety of people who have impacted her life.

Being a mother of five is in itself an education. Today she and her husband of forty three years work together in the construction of churches. God has given her a love for people and the desire to be an encourager along the journey of life.

Printed in the United States
1488600001B/277-345